Help Me Remember the Days of Creation

By Delphine Branon Bates

We'll help you remember!

Illustrated by Delphine Branon Bates and EsDesign

LifeSong Publishers
Somis, CA

ISBN: 978-0-9799116-3-7

Copyright 2010 by LifeSong Publishers

Published by LifeSong Publishers
P.O. Box 183, Somis, CA 93066-0183
805-504-3916
www.lifesongpublishers.com

Artwork and book design by Delphine Branon Bates and EsDesign.
Printed in South Korea

Library of Congress Cataloging-in-Publication Data

Bates, Delphine Branon, 1945-
  Help me remember the days of Creation / by Delphine Branon Bates ; illustrations by Delphine Branon Bates and EsDesign.
     p. cm. -- (Help me remember series ; 1)
  ISBN 978-0-9799116-3-7 (hardcover)
  1. Creation--Biblical teaching--Juvenile literature. 2. Christian education of children--Activity programs. I. EsDesign (Firm) II. Title.
  BS651.B285 2010
  222'.1109505--dc22
                              2010009684

Comments

"If someone were to ask me right now, 'What did God create on the 5th day?' or 'What's the 5th commandment?' or 'What's the 5th plague brought upon by the Egyptians?'...I would know the answer! And I would have Delphine Bates and her wonderfully imaginative books to thank for it. Honestly, she has given us, young and old alike, an ingenuous way to memorize the Ten Commandments, the Seven Days of Creation and, finally, the Ten Plagues of Egypt. What's more, she makes it so easy. You really must have these little treasures in your home and church library."

—Joni Eareckson Tada, Joni and Friends International Disability Center

"With unforgettable vivid imagery, Delphine Bates creatively provides wonderfully attractive and interesting resources for aiding kids (adults, too) to indelibly etch key biblical material, like the Days of Creation, the Egyptian Plagues, and the Ten Commandments, on their young minds. Every Christian parent should use these memorable materials with their children."

—Richard Mayhue, Th.D., Dean, The Master's Seminary, Sun Valley, CA

"Whether recalling a name, phone number or computer password, we often utilize word-pictures, acrostics, sound-alikes or visualization to help us remember. Amazingly, that's what the three "Help Me Remember" books do. By incorporating unique, creative and effective memory aids, Delphine Bates applies numerous mnemonic devices to tell the story of the character and purposes of God in the Bible. Refined over the years from teaching her own children and grandchildren, she now shares her secrets with us. Researched and accurately portrayed, learners of any age will find themselves easily grasping the central elements of these important parts of biblical history."

—Dr. Irv Busenitz, Vice President for Academic Administration, The Master's Seminary

To my husband, John, and our grandchildren-
JT, Curren, Whitney, Sierra, Tanner, Sheller, McKinley,
Wyatt, Ezra, Jonas, Andee, Silas, Olive, and Wilson.

"Choose today whom you will serve...
as for me and my family, we will serve the LORD."
Joshua 24:15

*Thank you to everyone who has shared their
ideas over the years, answered my
theological questions, or cheered me on.
And, most importantly, to the One who even
the wind and waves obey… my Savior.*

May I help you remember who He is?
John 20:31

Delphine

The Days of Creation
(partial quotes from the following verses)

Day 1: Genesis 1:3—Then God said, "Let there be light," and there was light.

Day 2: Genesis 1:6—And God said, "Let there be space between the waters, to separate water from water."

Day 3: Genesis 1:9—And God said, "Let the waters beneath the sky be gathered into one place so dry ground may appear."

Day 4: Genesis 1:14—And God said, "Let bright lights appear in the sky to separate the day from the night."

Day 5: Genesis 1:20—And God said, "Let the waters swarm with fish and other life. Let the skies be filled with birds of every kind."

Day 6: Genesis 1:24—And God said, "Let the earth bring forth every kind of animal – livestock, small animals, and wildlife."

Genesis 1:26—Then God said, "Let us make people in our image, to be like ourselves. They will be masters over all life."

Day 7: Genesis 2:2—On the seventh day, having finished his task, God rested from all his work.

Be sure to read the whole story of God's Creation in Genesis 1 and 2.

The First Day

God created light.
A candle gives us light.

Can you find a number 1 in this picture?

And can you find one of
anything in the picture?

Then God said, "Let there be light,"
and there was light.
—from Genesis 1:3—

The Second Day

God created the firmament. It is our sky. There was water above and below the firmament.

Can you find a number 2 in the picture?

And can you find two of anything in the picture?

And God said, "Let there be space between the waters, to separate water from water." —from Genesis 1:6—

The Third Day

God moved the waters to show the dry land.
The water and land make up our earth.

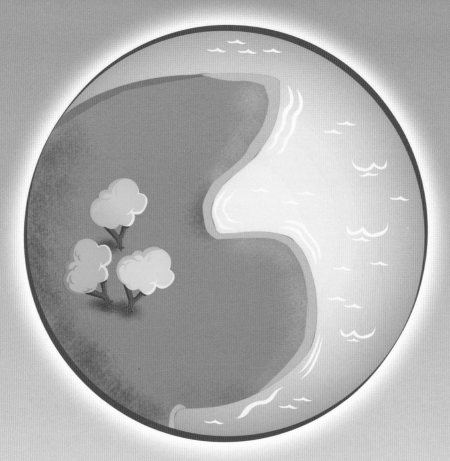

Can you find a number 3 in the picture?

And can you find three of
anything in the picture?

**And God said, "Let the waters beneath the
sky be gathered into one place so
dry ground may appear."
—from Genesis 1:9—**

The Fourth Day

God created the lights to shine down
upon the earth. The lights are the sun,
the moon, and the stars.

Can you find a number 4 in the picture?

And can you find four of
anything in the picture?

**And God said, "Let bright lights appear
in the sky to separate the day from the night."
—from Genesis 1:14—**

The Fifth Day

God created the fish and the birds. Look at the perch for the bird and the wave for the fish.

Can you find a number 5 in the picture?

And can you find five of
anything in the picture?

**And God said, "Let the waters swarm with fish
and other life. Let the skies be filled
with birds of every kind."
—from Genesis 1:20—**

The Sixth Day

God created animals and man.
Man was put in charge of all the animals.

Can you find a number 6 in the picture?

And can you find six of
anything in the picture?

**And God said, "Let the earth bring forth every kind
of animal – livestock, small animals, and wildlife."...
Then God said, "Let us make people in our image,
to be like ourselves. They will be masters
over all life." —from Genesis 1:24 and 26—**

The Seventh Day

God rested on the seventh day.
God didn't need to sleep,
but he enjoyed resting and looking
over all that he created.

Can you find a number 7 in the picture?

And can you find seven of
anything in the picture?

**On the seventh day, having finished his task,
God rested from all his work.
—from Genesis 2:2—**

The heavens are yours, the earth is yours;
everything in the world is yours—
you created it all.

— Psalm 89:11—

More Help Me Remember Books

Help Me Remember the Plagues of Egypt
by Delphine Bates

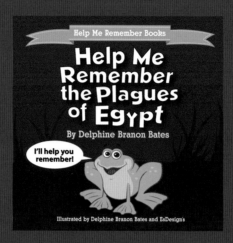

Help Me Remember the Ten Commandments
by Delphine Bates

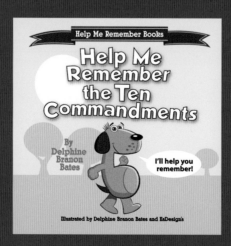

More LifeSong Books

Mr. Blue—A Job For You
by Laurie Donahue and Bryan Hintz
(with cut-out pieces for puzzle and play)

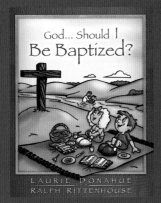

God...Should I Be Baptized?
by Laurie Donahue and Ralph Rittenhouse
(workbook for 8-12 years of age)

The Lord's Supper...Let's Get Ready!
by Laurie Donahue and Paul Phillipps
(workbook for 8-12 years of age)

Find these plus Bible Studies and
other books for adults at:
www.LifeSongPublishers.com
(or your favorite bookstore)
805-504-3916

Creation Counting Challenge

Day One: 1 flame, 1candle, 1 wick, 1 candle holder

Day Two: 2 bodies of water, 2 splashes above the lower water

Day Three: 3 trees

Day Four: 4 large stars, 4 eyes, 4 eyebrows

Day Five: 5 tail feathers and 5 head feathers on the bird, 5 spots on the bird's chest, 5 gills on the side of fish, 5 air bubbles

Day Six: 6 petals on the flower of the clown's hat, 6 buttons on the clown, 6 purple stripes on his sleeves, 6 orange stripes on his pant cuffs, 6 toes on the lion

Day Seven: 7 z's, the sun, moon, earth, and the large stars add up to 7